MY ORDERS

. . . .

www.sharonhowat.com

Why not tag me and your book on Instagram @sharon.howat

TOTAL INCOME CARRIED FORWARD

ORDER NUMBER	DATE OF ORDER	NAME	TOTAL
1			
2			
3			
4			
5			
6			
7			
8			
9			
10			
11			
12			
13			
14			
15			
16			
17			
18			
19			
20			
		TOTAL INCOME	

TOTAL INCOME CARRIED FORWARD

ORDER NUMBER	DATE OF ORDER	NAME	TOTAL
21			
22			
23			
24			
25			
26			
27			
28			
29			
30			
31			
32			
33			
34			
35			
36			
37			
38			
39			
40			
		TOTAL INCOME	

TOTAL INCOME CARRIED FORWARD

ORDER NUMBER	DATE OF ORDER	NAME	TOTAL
41			
42			
43			
44			
45			
46			
47			
48			
49			
50			
51			
52			
53			
54			
55			
56			
57			
58			
59			
60			
		TOTAL INCOME	

ORDER NUMBER	DATE OF ORDER	NAME	TOTAL
61			
62			
63			
64			
65			
66			
67			
68			
69			
70			
71			
72			
73			
74			
75			
76			
77			
78			
79			
80			
		TOTAL INCOME	

TOTAL INCOME CARRIED FORWARD

ORDER NUMBER	DATE OF ORDER	NAME	TOTAL
81			
82			
83			
84			
85			
86			
87			
88			
89			
90			
91			
92			
93			
94			
95			
96			
97			
98			
99			
100			
		TOTAL INCOME	

TOTAL INCOME CARRIED FORWARD

ORDER NUMBER	DATE OF ORDER	NAME	TOTAL
101			
102			
103			
104			
105			
106			
107			
108			
109			
110			
111			
112			
113			
114			
115			
116			
117			
118			
119			
120			
		TOTAL INCOME	

ORDER NUMBER	DATE OF ORDER	NAME	TOTAL
121			
122			
123			
124			
125			
126			
127			
128			
129			
130			
131			
132			
133			
134			
135			
136			
137			
138			
139			
140			
		TOTAL INCOME	

ORDER NUMBER	DATE OF ORDER	NAME	TOTAL
141			
142			
143			
144			
145			
146			
147			
148			
149			
150			
151			
152			
153			
154			
155			
156			
157			
158			
159			
160			
		TOTAL INCOME	

ORDER NUMBER	DATE OF ORDER	NAME	TOTAL
161			
162			
163			
164			
165			
166			
167			
168			
169			
170			
171			
172			
173			
174			
175			
176			
177			
178			
179			
180			
		TOTAL INCOME	

ORDER NUMBER	DATE OF ORDER	NAME	TOTAL
181			
182			
183			
184			
185			
186			
187			
188			
189			
190			
191			
192			
193			
194			
195			
196			
197			
198			
199			
200			
		TOTAL INCOME	

Name:	Order No: 1	Date of Order:
Address:		Date Placed:

Post ◯ Collect ◯ Deliver ◯

Contacted via: Paid Via: Tracking No:

[Instagram] [Facebook] [Twitter] [Snapchat]   [PayPal] [Globe] [Cash]   Samples Sent:

◯ ◯ ◯ ◯   ◯ ◯ ◯

PRODUCT	FRAGRANCE	QTY	TOTAL
Notes:		Postage	
		Total	

Name:	Order No: 2	Date of Order:
Address:		Date Placed:

Post ◯ Collect ◯ Deliver ◯

Contacted via: Paid Via: Tracking No:

[Instagram] [Facebook] [Twitter] [Snapchat]   [PayPal] [Globe] [Cash]   Samples Sent:

◯ ◯ ◯ ◯   ◯ ◯ ◯

PRODUCT	FRAGRANCE	QTY	TOTAL
Notes:		Postage	
		Total	

Name: Order No: Date of Order:

Address:
                                                        Date Placed:
Post ◯   Collect ◯   Deliver ◯

Contacted via: Paid Via: Tracking No:

[Instagram] [f] [Twitter] [Snapchat]   [P] [🌐] [💵]   Samples Sent:

◯   ◯   ◯   ◯   ◯   ◯   ◯

PRODUCT	FRAGRANCE	QTY	TOTAL

Notes: Postage
                                          Total

Name: Order No: Date of Order:

Address:
                                                        Date Placed:
Post ◯   Collect ◯   Deliver ◯

Contacted via: Paid Via: Tracking No:

[Instagram] [f] [Twitter] [Snapchat]   [P] [🌐] [💵]   Samples Sent:

◯   ◯   ◯   ◯   ◯   ◯   ◯

PRODUCT	FRAGRANCE	QTY	TOTAL

Notes: Postage
                                          Total

Name:		Order No:		Date of Order:
Address:				Date Placed:
Post ◯ Collect ◯ Deliver ◯				
Contacted via:		Paid Via:		Tracking No:
[icons] ◯ ◯ ◯ ◯		[icons] ◯ ◯ ◯		Samples Sent:

PRODUCT	FRAGRANCE	QTY	TOTAL
Notes:		Postage	
		Total	

Name:		Order No:		Date of Order:
Address:				Date Placed:
Post ◯ Collect ◯ Deliver ◯				
Contacted via:		Paid Via:		Tracking No:
[icons] ◯ ◯ ◯ ◯		[icons] ◯ ◯ ◯		Samples Sent:

PRODUCT	FRAGRANCE	QTY	TOTAL
Notes:		Postage	
		Total	

Name:		Order No:		Date of Order:

Address:

Post ⬭ Collect ⬭ Deliver ⬭

Date Placed:

Contacted via:

Paid Via:

Tracking No:

Samples Sent:

PRODUCT	FRAGRANCE	QTY	TOTAL

Notes:

Postage	
Total	

Name:		Order No:		Date of Order:

Address:

Post ⬭ Collect ⬭ Deliver ⬭

Date Placed:

Contacted via:

Paid Via:

Tracking No:

Samples Sent:

PRODUCT	FRAGRANCE	QTY	TOTAL

Notes:

Postage	
Total	

Name:	Order No:	Date of Order:

Address:

Post ⬭   Collect ⬭   Deliver ⬭

Date Placed:

Contacted via: Paid Via:

Tracking No:

Samples Sent:

⬭ ⬭ ⬭ ⬭   ⬭ ⬭ ⬭

PRODUCT	FRAGRANCE	QTY	TOTAL

Notes:

	Postage	
	Total	

Name:	Order No:	Date of Order:

Address:

Post ⬭   Collect ⬭   Deliver ⬭

Date Placed:

Contacted via: Paid Via:

Tracking No:

Samples Sent:

⬭ ⬭ ⬭ ⬭   ⬭ ⬭ ⬭

PRODUCT	FRAGRANCE	QTY	TOTAL

Notes:

	Postage	
	Total	

Name:	Order No:	Date of Order:
Address:		Date Placed:
Post ◯ Collect ◯ Deliver ◯		
Contacted via:	Paid Via:	Tracking No:
[Instagram] [Facebook] [Twitter] [Snapchat]	[PayPal] [Globe] [Cash]	
◯ ◯ ◯ ◯	◯ ◯ ◯	Samples Sent:

PRODUCT	FRAGRANCE	QTY	TOTAL

Notes:

	Postage	
	Total	

Name:	Order No:	Date of Order:
Address:		Date Placed:
Post ◯ Collect ◯ Deliver ◯		
Contacted via:	Paid Via:	Tracking No:
[Instagram] [Facebook] [Twitter] [Snapchat]	[PayPal] [Globe] [Cash]	
◯ ◯ ◯ ◯	◯ ◯ ◯	Samples Sent:

PRODUCT	FRAGRANCE	QTY	TOTAL

Notes:

	Postage	
	Total	

Name: Order No: Date of Order:

Address:
                                                            Date Placed:
Post ◯   Collect ◯   Deliver ◯

Contacted via: Paid Via: Tracking No:

[Instagram] [Facebook] [Twitter] [Snapchat]   [PayPal] [Globe] [Cash]
                                                            Samples Sent:
◯   ◯   ◯   ◯   ◯   ◯   ◯

PRODUCT	FRAGRANCE	QTY	TOTAL

Notes: Postage | |
                                                Total | |

Name: Order No: Date of Order:

Address:
                                                            Date Placed:
Post ◯   Collect ◯   Deliver ◯

Contacted via: Paid Via: Tracking No:

[Instagram] [Facebook] [Twitter] [Snapchat]   [PayPal] [Globe] [Cash]
                                                            Samples Sent:
◯   ◯   ◯   ◯   ◯   ◯   ◯

PRODUCT	FRAGRANCE	QTY	TOTAL

Notes: Postage | |
                                                Total | |

Name:	Order No:	Date of Order:
Address:		Date Placed:
Post ◯ Collect ◯ Deliver ◯		
Contacted via:	Paid Via:	Tracking No:
◯ ◯ ◯ ◯	◯ ◯ ◯	Samples Sent:

PRODUCT	FRAGRANCE	QTY	TOTAL

Notes:

Postage	
Total	

Name:	Order No:	Date of Order:
Address:		Date Placed:
Post ◯ Collect ◯ Deliver ◯		
Contacted via:	Paid Via:	Tracking No:
◯ ◯ ◯ ◯	◯ ◯ ◯	Samples Sent:

PRODUCT	FRAGRANCE	QTY	TOTAL

Notes:

Postage	
Total	

Name: **Order No:**   **Date of Order:**

Address:

Date Placed:

Post ( )   Collect ( )   Deliver ( )

Contacted via: Paid Via: **Tracking No:**

[Instagram] [Facebook] [Twitter] [Snapchat]   [PayPal] [Web] [Cash]

( )   ( )   ( )   ( )   ( )   ( )   ( )

Samples Sent:

PRODUCT	FRAGRANCE	QTY	TOTAL

Notes: Postage

                      Total

Name: **Order No:**   **Date of Order:**

Address:

Date Placed:

Post ( )   Collect ( )   Deliver ( )

Contacted via: Paid Via: **Tracking No:**

[Instagram] [Facebook] [Twitter] [Snapchat]   [PayPal] [Web] [Cash]

( )   ( )   ( )   ( )   ( )   ( )   ( )

Samples Sent:

PRODUCT	FRAGRANCE	QTY	TOTAL

Notes: Postage

                      Total

Name:	Order No:	Date of Order:	
Address:		Date Placed:	
Post ⬭ Collect ⬭ Deliver ⬭			
Contacted via:	Paid Via:	Tracking No:	
[Instagram] [Facebook] [Twitter] [Snapchat]	[PayPal] [Web] [Cash]	Samples Sent:	
⬭ ⬭ ⬭ ⬭	⬭ ⬭ ⬭		

PRODUCT	FRAGRANCE	QTY	TOTAL

Notes:	Postage	
	Total	

Name:	Order No:	Date of Order:	
Address:		Date Placed:	
Post ⬭ Collect ⬭ Deliver ⬭			
Contacted via:	Paid Via:	Tracking No:	
[Instagram] [Facebook] [Twitter] [Snapchat]	[PayPal] [Web] [Cash]	Samples Sent:	
⬭ ⬭ ⬭ ⬭	⬭ ⬭ ⬭		

PRODUCT	FRAGRANCE	QTY	TOTAL

Notes:	Postage	
	Total	

Name:		Order No:		Date of Order:
Address:				Date Placed:
Post ◯　Collect ◯　Deliver ◯				
Contacted via:		Paid Via:		Tracking No:
[Instagram] [Facebook] [Twitter] [Snapchat]		[PayPal] [Globe] [Cash]		Samples Sent:
◯　◯　◯　◯		◯　◯　◯		

PRODUCT	FRAGRANCE	QTY	TOTAL

Notes:

Postage	
Total	

Name:		Order No:		Date of Order:
Address:				Date Placed:
Post ◯　Collect ◯　Deliver ◯				
Contacted via:		Paid Via:		Tracking No:
[Instagram] [Facebook] [Twitter] [Snapchat]		[PayPal] [Globe] [Cash]		Samples Sent:
◯　◯　◯　◯		◯　◯　◯		

PRODUCT	FRAGRANCE	QTY	TOTAL

Notes:

Postage	
Total	

Name:	Order No:	Date of Order:
Address:		

Post ◯　　Collect ◯　　Deliver ◯

Date Placed:

Contacted via:　　　　　　　　Paid Via:

Tracking No:

◯　◯　◯　◯　　　◯　◯　◯

Samples Sent:

PRODUCT	FRAGRANCE	QTY	TOTAL

Notes:

Postage	
Total	

Name:	Order No:	Date of Order:
Address:		

Post ◯　　Collect ◯　　Deliver ◯

Date Placed:

Contacted via:　　　　　　　　Paid Via:

Tracking No:

◯　◯　◯　◯　　　◯　◯　◯

Samples Sent:

PRODUCT	FRAGRANCE	QTY	TOTAL

Notes:

Postage	
Total	

Name: Order No: Date of Order:

Address:

Post ⬭   Collect ⬭   Deliver ⬭   Date Placed:

Contacted via: Paid Via:

📷 f 🐦 👻   P 🌐 💲   Tracking No:

⬭   ⬭   ⬭   ⬭   ⬭   ⬭   ⬭   Samples Sent:

PRODUCT	FRAGRANCE	QTY	TOTAL

Notes: Postage |
                                                    Total |

Name: Order No: Date of Order:

Address:

Post ⬭   Collect ⬭   Deliver ⬭   Date Placed:

Contacted via: Paid Via:

📷 f 🐦 👻   P 🌐 💲   Tracking No:

⬭   ⬭   ⬭   ⬭   ⬭   ⬭   ⬭   Samples Sent:

PRODUCT	FRAGRANCE	QTY	TOTAL

Notes: Postage |
                                                    Total |

Name: Order No: Date of Order:

Address:
                                             Date Placed:
Post ◯   Collect ◯   Deliver ◯

Contacted via: Paid Via: Tracking No:

[Instagram] [Facebook] [Twitter] [Snapchat]   [PayPal] [Web] [Cash]

                                             Samples Sent:
◯   ◯   ◯   ◯   ◯   ◯   ◯

PRODUCT	FRAGRANCE	QTY	TOTAL

Notes: Postage | |
                                        Total | |

Name: Order No: Date of Order:

Address:
                                             Date Placed:
Post ◯   Collect ◯   Deliver ◯

Contacted via: Paid Via: Tracking No:

[Instagram] [Facebook] [Twitter] [Snapchat]   [PayPal] [Web] [Cash]

                                             Samples Sent:
◯   ◯   ◯   ◯   ◯   ◯   ◯

PRODUCT	FRAGRANCE	QTY	TOTAL

Notes: Postage | |
                                        Total | |

Name: Order No: Date of Order:

Address:
                                                      Date Placed:
Post ( )   Collect ( )   Deliver ( )

Contacted via: Paid Via: Tracking No:

[Instagram] [Facebook] [Twitter] [Snapchat]   [PayPal] [Web] [Cash]
                                                      Samples Sent:
( )   ( )   ( )   ( )   ( )   ( )   ( )

PRODUCT	FRAGRANCE	QTY	TOTAL

Notes: Postage | |
                                               Total | |

Name: Order No: Date of Order:

Address:
                                                      Date Placed:
Post ( )   Collect ( )   Deliver ( )

Contacted via: Paid Via: Tracking No:

[Instagram] [Facebook] [Twitter] [Snapchat]   [PayPal] [Web] [Cash]
                                                      Samples Sent:
( )   ( )   ( )   ( )   ( )   ( )   ( )

PRODUCT	FRAGRANCE	QTY	TOTAL

Notes: Postage | |
                                               Total | |

Name: Order No: Date of Order:

Address:
                                                Date Placed:
Post ◯   Collect ◯   Deliver ◯

Contacted via: Paid Via: Tracking No:

[Instagram] [Facebook] [Twitter] [Snapchat]   [PayPal] [Globe] [Cash]   Samples Sent:
   ◯   ◯   ◯   ◯   ◯   ◯   ◯

PRODUCT	FRAGRANCE	QTY	TOTAL

Notes: Postage | |
                                          Total | |

Name: Order No: Date of Order:

Address:
                                                Date Placed:
Post ◯   Collect ◯   Deliver ◯

Contacted via: Paid Via: Tracking No:

[Instagram] [Facebook] [Twitter] [Snapchat]   [PayPal] [Globe] [Cash]   Samples Sent:
   ◯   ◯   ◯   ◯   ◯   ◯   ◯

PRODUCT	FRAGRANCE	QTY	TOTAL

Notes: Postage | |
                                          Total | |

Name: Order No: Date of Order:

Address:
                                                                Date Placed:
Post ◯   Collect ◯   Deliver ◯

Contacted via: Paid Via: Tracking No:

[Instagram] [Facebook] [Twitter] [Snapchat]   [PayPal] [Globe] [Cash]   Samples Sent:

◯   ◯   ◯   ◯   ◯   ◯   ◯

PRODUCT	FRAGRANCE	QTY	TOTAL

Notes: Postage | |
                                                Total | |

Name: Order No: Date of Order:

Address:
                                                                Date Placed:
Post ◯   Collect ◯   Deliver ◯

Contacted via: Paid Via: Tracking No:

[Instagram] [Facebook] [Twitter] [Snapchat]   [PayPal] [Globe] [Cash]   Samples Sent:

◯   ◯   ◯   ◯   ◯   ◯   ◯

PRODUCT	FRAGRANCE	QTY	TOTAL

Notes: Postage | |
                                                Total | |

Name: Order No: Date of Order:

Address:
                                                                          Date Placed:
Post ⭕   Collect ⭕   Deliver ⭕

Contacted via: **Paid Via:**   Tracking No:

[Instagram] [Facebook] [Twitter] [Snapchat]   [PayPal] [Globe] [Cash]

⭕   ⭕   ⭕   ⭕   ⭕   ⭕   ⭕   Samples Sent:

PRODUCT	FRAGRANCE	QTY	TOTAL

Notes: Postage | |

                                                        Total | |

Name: Order No: Date of Order:

Address:
                                                                          Date Placed:
Post ⭕   Collect ⭕   Deliver ⭕

Contacted via: **Paid Via:**   Tracking No:

[Instagram] [Facebook] [Twitter] [Snapchat]   [PayPal] [Globe] [Cash]

⭕   ⭕   ⭕   ⭕   ⭕   ⭕   ⭕   Samples Sent:

PRODUCT	FRAGRANCE	QTY	TOTAL

Notes: Postage | |

                                                        Total | |

Name: **Order No:**   **Date of Order:**

Address:

Date Placed:

Post ◯   Collect ◯   Deliver ◯

Contacted via: Paid Via:

Tracking No:

◯   ◯   ◯   ◯   ◯   ◯   ◯

Samples Sent:

PRODUCT	FRAGRANCE	QTY	TOTAL
Notes:		Postage	
		Total	

Name: **Order No:**   **Date of Order:**

Address:

Date Placed:

Post ◯   Collect ◯   Deliver ◯

Contacted via: Paid Via:

Tracking No:

◯   ◯   ◯   ◯   ◯   ◯   ◯

Samples Sent:

PRODUCT	FRAGRANCE	QTY	TOTAL
Notes:		Postage	
		Total	

Name: Order No: Date of Order:

Address:

Date Placed:

Post ⬭   Collect ⬭   Deliver ⬭

Contacted via: Paid Via: Tracking No:

[Instagram] [Facebook] [Twitter] [Snapchat]   [PayPal] [Globe] [Cash]

Samples Sent:

⬭   ⬭   ⬭   ⬭   ⬭   ⬭   ⬭

PRODUCT	FRAGRANCE	QTY	TOTAL

Notes: Postage | |
                                          Total | |

Name: Order No: Date of Order:

Address:

Date Placed:

Post ⬭   Collect ⬭   Deliver ⬭

Contacted via: Paid Via: Tracking No:

[Instagram] [Facebook] [Twitter] [Snapchat]   [PayPal] [Globe] [Cash]

Samples Sent:

⬭   ⬭   ⬭   ⬭   ⬭   ⬭   ⬭

PRODUCT	FRAGRANCE	QTY	TOTAL

Notes: Postage | |
                                          Total | |

Name:	Order No:	Date of Order:

Address:

Post ⬭　　Collect ⬭　　Deliver ⬭

Date Placed:

Contacted via:　　　　　Paid Via:

Tracking No:

⬭　　⬭　　⬭　　⬭　　　⬭　　⬭　　⬭

Samples Sent:

PRODUCT	FRAGRANCE	QTY	TOTAL

Notes:

Postage	
Total	

Name:	Order No:	Date of Order:

Address:

Post ⬭　　Collect ⬭　　Deliver ⬭

Date Placed:

Contacted via:　　　· Paid Via:

Tracking No:

⬭　　⬭　　⬭　　⬭　　　⬭　　⬭　　⬭

Samples Sent:

PRODUCT	FRAGRANCE	QTY	TOTAL

Notes:

Postage	
Total	

Name: Order No:

Date of Order:

Address:

Date Placed:

Post ⭕   Collect ⭕   Deliver ⭕

Contacted via: **Paid Via:**   **Tracking No:**

⭕ ⭕ ⭕ ⭕   ⭕ ⭕ ⭕   **Samples Sent:**

PRODUCT	FRAGRANCE	QTY	TOTAL

Notes: Postage

                                                    Total

Name: Order No:

Date of Order:

Address:

Date Placed:

Post ⭕   Collect ⭕   Deliver ⭕

Contacted via: **Paid Via:**   **Tracking No:**

⭕ ⭕ ⭕ ⭕   ⭕ ⭕ ⭕   **Samples Sent:**

PRODUCT	FRAGRANCE	QTY	TOTAL

Notes: Postage

                                                    Total

Name: Order No: Date of Order:

Address:
                                                      Date Placed:
Post ◯   Collect ◯   Deliver ◯

Contacted via: Paid Via: Tracking No:

◯   ◯   ◯   ◯   ◯   ◯   ◯   Samples Sent:

PRODUCT	FRAGRANCE	QTY	TOTAL

Notes: Postage | |
                                                          Total | |

Name: Order No: Date of Order:

Address:
                                                      Date Placed:
Post ◯   Collect ◯   Deliver ◯

Contacted via: Paid Via: Tracking No:

◯   ◯   ◯   ◯   ◯   ◯   ◯   Samples Sent:

PRODUCT	FRAGRANCE	QTY	TOTAL

Notes: Postage | |
                                                          Total | |

Name: Order No:

Address:

Post ⬭   Collect ⬭   Deliver ⬭

Contacted via: **Paid Via:**

🔲 🔲 🔲 🔲   🔲 🔲 🔲

⬭   ⬭   ⬭   ⬭   ⬭   ⬭   ⬭

Date of Order:

Date Placed:

Tracking No:

Samples Sent:

PRODUCT	FRAGRANCE	QTY	TOTAL

Notes:

Postage | |
Total | |

Name: Order No:

Address:

Post ⬭   Collect ⬭   Deliver ⬭

Contacted via: **Paid Via:**

🔲 🔲 🔲 🔲   🔲 🔲 🔲

⬭   ⬭   ⬭   ⬭   ⬭   ⬭   ⬭

Date of Order:

Date Placed:

Tracking No:

Samples Sent:

PRODUCT	FRAGRANCE	QTY	TOTAL

Notes:

Postage | |
Total | |

Name: Order No: Date of Order:

Address:

Date Placed:

Post ◯   Collect ◯   Deliver ◯

Contacted via: Paid Via: Tracking No:

📷	f	🐦	👻	P	🌐	💵	Samples Sent:
◯	◯	◯	◯	◯	◯	◯	

PRODUCT	FRAGRANCE	QTY	TOTAL

Notes: Postage |
Total

Name: Order No: Date of Order:

Address:

Date Placed:

Post ◯   Collect ◯   Deliver ◯

Contacted via: Paid Via: Tracking No:

📷	f	🐦	👻	P	🌐	💵	Samples Sent:
◯	◯	◯	◯	◯	◯	◯	

PRODUCT	FRAGRANCE	QTY	TOTAL

Notes: Postage |
Total

Name: Order No: Date of Order:

Address:
                                                                         Date Placed:
Post ◯   Collect ◯   Deliver ◯

Contacted via: Paid Via: Tracking No:

▢ ▢ ▢ ▢   ▢ ▢ ▢   Samples Sent:

◯   ◯   ◯   ◯   ◯   ◯   ◯

PRODUCT	FRAGRANCE	QTY	TOTAL

Notes: Postage

                                                    Total

Name: Order No: Date of Order:

Address:
                                                                         Date Placed:
Post ◯   Collect ◯   Deliver ◯

Contacted via: Paid Via: Tracking No:

▢ ▢ ▢ ▢   ▢ ▢ ▢   Samples Sent:

◯   ◯   ◯   ◯   ◯   ◯   ◯

PRODUCT	FRAGRANCE	QTY	TOTAL

Notes: Postage

                                                    Total

Name:

Order No:

Date of Order:

Address:

Date Placed:

Post ◯   Collect ◯   Deliver ◯

Tracking No:

Contacted via: **Paid Via:**

Samples Sent:

◯   ◯   ◯   ◯   ◯   ◯   ◯

PRODUCT	FRAGRANCE	QTY	TOTAL

Notes: Postage

Total

Name:

Order No:

Date of Order:

Address:

Date Placed:

Post ◯   Collect ◯   Deliver ◯

Tracking No:

Contacted via: **Paid Via:**

Samples Sent:

◯   ◯   ◯   ◯   ◯   ◯   ◯

PRODUCT	FRAGRANCE	QTY	TOTAL

Notes: Postage

Total

Name: **Order No:**   **Date of Order:**

Address:

Date Placed:

Post ◯   Collect ◯   Deliver ◯

Contacted via: **Paid Via:**   **Tracking No:**

[Instagram] [Facebook] [Twitter] [Snapchat]   [PayPal] [Web] [Cash]

Samples Sent:

◯   ◯   ◯   ◯   ◯   ◯   ◯

PRODUCT	FRAGRANCE	QTY	TOTAL

Notes: Postage

Total

Name: **Order No:**   **Date of Order:**

Address:

Date Placed:

Post ◯   Collect ◯   Deliver ◯

Contacted via: **Paid Via:**   **Tracking No:**

[Instagram] [Facebook] [Twitter] [Snapchat]   [PayPal] [Web] [Cash]

Samples Sent:

◯   ◯   ◯   ◯   ◯   ◯   ◯

PRODUCT	FRAGRANCE	QTY	TOTAL

Notes: Postage

Total

Name: Order No: Date of Order:

Address:

Date Placed:

Post ◯   Collect ◯   Deliver ◯

Contacted via: Paid Via: Tracking No:

[Instagram] [Facebook] [Twitter] [Snapchat]   [PayPal] [Web] [Cash]

Samples Sent:

◯   ◯   ◯   ◯   ◯   ◯   ◯

PRODUCT	FRAGRANCE	QTY	TOTAL

Notes: Postage

Total

Name: Order No: Date of Order:

Address:

Date Placed:

Post ◯   Collect ◯   Deliver ◯

Contacted via: Paid Via: Tracking No:

[Instagram] [Facebook] [Twitter] [Snapchat]   [PayPal] [Web] [Cash]

Samples Sent:

◯   ◯   ◯   ◯   ◯   ◯   ◯

PRODUCT	FRAGRANCE	QTY	TOTAL

Notes: Postage

Total

Name: Order No: Date of Order:

Address:
                                                            Date Placed:
Post ◯   Collect ◯   Deliver ◯

Contacted via: Paid Via: Tracking No:

[Instagram] [f] [Twitter] [Snapchat]   [P] [globe] [$]
                                                            Samples Sent:
◯   ◯   ◯   ◯   ◯   ◯   ◯

PRODUCT	FRAGRANCE	QTY	TOTAL

Notes: Postage

                                              Total

Name: Order No: Date of Order:

Address:
                                                            Date Placed:
Post ◯   Collect ◯   Deliver ◯

Contacted via: Paid Via: Tracking No:

[Instagram] [f] [Twitter] [Snapchat]   [P] [globe] [$]
                                                            Samples Sent:
◯   ◯   ◯   ◯   ◯   ◯   ◯

PRODUCT	FRAGRANCE	QTY	TOTAL

Notes: Postage

                                              Total

Name: Order No: Date of Order:

Address:
                                                                                Date Placed:
Post ◯   Collect ◯   Deliver ◯

Contacted via: **Paid Via:**   Tracking No:

[Instagram] [Facebook] [Twitter] [Snapchat]   [PayPal] [Web] [Cash]

◯   ◯   ◯   ◯   ◯   ◯   ◯   Samples Sent:

PRODUCT	FRAGRANCE	QTY	TOTAL

Notes: Postage | |
                                                        Total | |

Name: Order No: Date of Order:

Address:
                                                                                Date Placed:
Post ◯   Collect ◯   Deliver ◯

Contacted via: **Paid Via:**   Tracking No:

[Instagram] [Facebook] [Twitter] [Snapchat]   [PayPal] [Web] [Cash]

◯   ◯   ◯   ◯   ◯   ◯   ◯   Samples Sent:

PRODUCT	FRAGRANCE	QTY	TOTAL

Notes: Postage | |
                                                        Total | |

Name: Order No: Date of Order:

Address:
                                                  Date Placed:
Post ◯   Collect ◯   Deliver ◯

Contacted via: Paid Via: Tracking No:

[Instagram] [Facebook] [Twitter] [Snapchat]   [PayPal] [Globe] [Cash]
                                                  Samples Sent:
   ◯   ◯   ◯   ◯   ◯   ◯   ◯

PRODUCT	FRAGRANCE	QTY	TOTAL

Notes: Postage

                                          Total

Name: Order No: Date of Order:

Address:
                                                  Date Placed:
Post ◯   Collect ◯   Deliver ◯

Contacted via: Paid Via: Tracking No:

[Instagram] [Facebook] [Twitter] [Snapchat]   [PayPal] [Globe] [Cash]
                                                  Samples Sent:
   ◯   ◯   ◯   ◯   ◯   ◯   ◯

PRODUCT	FRAGRANCE	QTY	TOTAL

Notes: Postage

                                          Total

Name: Order No: Date of Order:

Address:
                                                          Date Placed:
Post ◯   Collect ◯   Deliver ◯

Contacted via: Paid Via: Tracking No:

[Instagram] [Facebook] [Twitter] [Snapchat]   [PayPal] [Globe] [Cash]
                                                          Samples Sent:
◯   ◯   ◯   ◯   ◯   ◯   ◯

PRODUCT	FRAGRANCE	QTY	TOTAL

Notes: Postage | |
                                                Total | |

Name: Order No: Date of Order:

Address:
                                                          Date Placed:
Post ◯   Collect ◯   Deliver ◯

Contacted via: Paid Via: Tracking No:

[Instagram] [Facebook] [Twitter] [Snapchat]   [PayPal] [Globe] [Cash]
                                                          Samples Sent:
◯   ◯   ◯   ◯   ◯   ◯   ◯

PRODUCT	FRAGRANCE	QTY	TOTAL

Notes: Postage | |
                                                Total | |

Name: Order No: Date of Order:

Address:

Post ◯   Collect ◯   Deliver ◯   Date Placed:

Contacted via: Paid Via: Tracking No:

[Instagram] [Facebook] [Twitter] [Snapchat]   [PayPal] [Globe] [Cash]

◯   ◯   ◯   ◯   ◯   ◯   ◯   Samples Sent:

PRODUCT	FRAGRANCE	QTY	TOTAL

Notes: Postage | |
                                  Total | |

Name: Order No: Date of Order:

Address:

Post ◯   Collect ◯   Deliver ◯   Date Placed:

Contacted via: Paid Via: Tracking No:

[Instagram] [Facebook] [Twitter] [Snapchat]   [PayPal] [Globe] [Cash]

◯   ◯   ◯   ◯   ◯   ◯   ◯   Samples Sent:

PRODUCT	FRAGRANCE	QTY	TOTAL

Notes: Postage | |
                                  Total | |

Name:

Order No:

Date of Order:

Address:

Date Placed:

Post ( )   Collect ( )   Deliver ( )

Contacted via: **Paid Via:**

Tracking No:

( ) ( ) ( ) ( )   ( ) ( ) ( )

Samples Sent:

PRODUCT	FRAGRANCE	QTY	TOTAL

Notes:

		Postage	
		Total	

Name:

Order No:

Date of Order:

Address:

Date Placed:

Post ( )   Collect ( )   Deliver ( )

Contacted via: **Paid Via:**

Tracking No:

( ) ( ) ( ) ( )   ( ) ( ) ( )

Samples Sent:

PRODUCT	FRAGRANCE	QTY	TOTAL

Notes:

		Postage	
		Total	

Name:	Order No:	Date of Order:

Address:

Post ◯   Collect ◯   Deliver ◯

Date Placed:

Contacted via: Paid Via:

Tracking No:

◯ ◯ ◯ ◯   ◯ ◯ ◯

Samples Sent:

PRODUCT	FRAGRANCE	QTY	TOTAL

Notes:

Postage	
Total	

Name:	Order No:	Date of Order:

Address:

Post ◯   Collect ◯   Deliver ◯

Date Placed:

Contacted via: Paid Via:

Tracking No:

◯ ◯ ◯ ◯   ◯ ◯ ◯

Samples Sent:

PRODUCT	FRAGRANCE	QTY	TOTAL

Notes:

Postage	
Total	

Name: Order No: Date of Order:

Address:
                                                                                Date Placed:
Post ◯   Collect ◯   Deliver ◯

Contacted via: Paid Via: Tracking No:

[Instagram] [Facebook] [Twitter] [Snapchat]   [PayPal] [Globe] [Cash]

◯   ◯   ◯   ◯   ◯   ◯   ◯   Samples Sent:

PRODUCT	FRAGRANCE	QTY	TOTAL

Notes: Postage | |
                                                                Total | |

Name: Order No: Date of Order:

Address:
                                                                                Date Placed:
Post ◯   Collect ◯   Deliver ◯

Contacted via: Paid Via: Tracking No:

[Instagram] [Facebook] [Twitter] [Snapchat]   [PayPal] [Globe] [Cash]

◯   ◯   ◯   ◯   ◯   ◯   ◯   Samples Sent:

PRODUCT	FRAGRANCE	QTY	TOTAL

Notes: Postage | |
                                                                Total | |

Name: Order No:

Address:

Post ◯   Collect ◯   Deliver ◯

Contacted via: **Paid Via:**

[Instagram] [Facebook] [Twitter] [Snapchat]   [PayPal] [Web] [Cash]
◯   ◯   ◯   ◯   ◯   ◯   ◯

Date of Order:

Date Placed:

Tracking No:

Samples Sent:

PRODUCT	FRAGRANCE	QTY	TOTAL

Notes: Postage | |

                                                Total | |

Name: Order No:

Address:

Post ◯   Collect ◯   Deliver ◯

Contacted via: **Paid Via:**

[Instagram] [Facebook] [Twitter] [Snapchat]   [PayPal] [Web] [Cash]
◯   ◯   ◯   ◯   ◯   ◯   ◯

Date of Order:

Date Placed:

Tracking No:

Samples Sent:

PRODUCT	FRAGRANCE	QTY	TOTAL

Notes: Postage | |

                                                Total | |

Name: Order No: Date of Order:

Address:
                                                      Date Placed:
Post ⬭   Collect ⬭   Deliver ⬭

Contacted via: Paid Via: Tracking No:

[Instagram] [f] [Twitter] [Snapchat]   [P] [🌐] [💵]

⬭   ⬭   ⬭   ⬭   ⬭   ⬭   ⬭   Samples Sent:

PRODUCT	FRAGRANCE	QTY	TOTAL

Notes: Postage | |
                                          Total | |

Name: Order No: Date of Order:

Address:
                                                      Date Placed:
Post ⬭   Collect ⬭   Deliver ⬭

Contacted via: Paid Via: Tracking No:

[Instagram] [f] [Twitter] [Snapchat]   [P] [🌐] [💵]

⬭   ⬭   ⬭   ⬭   ⬭   ⬭   ⬭   Samples Sent:

PRODUCT	FRAGRANCE	QTY	TOTAL

Notes: Postage | |
                                          Total | |

Name:	Order No:	Date of Order:
Address:		
Post ◯ Collect ◯ Deliver ◯		Date Placed:
Contacted via:	Paid Via:	Tracking No:
📷 f 🐦 👻	P 🌐 💵	
◯ ◯ ◯ ◯	◯ ◯ ◯	Samples Sent:

PRODUCT	FRAGRANCE	QTY	TOTAL

Notes:

Postage	
Total	

Name:	Order No:	Date of Order:
Address:		
Post ◯ Collect ◯ Deliver ◯		Date Placed:
Contacted via:	Paid Via:	Tracking No:
📷 f 🐦 👻	P 🌐 💵	
◯ ◯ ◯ ◯	◯ ◯ ◯	Samples Sent:

PRODUCT	FRAGRANCE	QTY	TOTAL

Notes:

Postage	
Total	

Name: Order No: Date of Order:

Address:
                                                    Date Placed:
Post ◯   Collect ◯   Deliver ◯

Contacted via: **Paid Via:**   Tracking No:

[Instagram] [Facebook] [Twitter] [Snapchat]   [PayPal] [Globe] [Cash]   Samples Sent:

◯   ◯   ◯   ◯   ◯   ◯   ◯

PRODUCT	FRAGRANCE	QTY	TOTAL

Notes: Postage | |
                                          Total | |

Name: Order No: Date of Order:

Address:
                                                    Date Placed:
Post ◯   Collect ◯   Deliver ◯

Contacted via: **Paid Via:**   Tracking No:

[Instagram] [Facebook] [Twitter] [Snapchat]   [PayPal] [Globe] [Cash]   Samples Sent:

◯   ◯   ◯   ◯   ◯   ◯   ◯

PRODUCT	FRAGRANCE	QTY	TOTAL

Notes: Postage | |
                                          Total | |

Name: Order No: Date of Order:

Address:

Date Placed:

Post ⬭   Collect ⬭   Deliver ⬭

Tracking No:

Contacted via: Paid Via:

Samples Sent:

⬭   ⬭   ⬭   ⬭   ⬭   ⬭   ⬭

PRODUCT	FRAGRANCE	QTY	TOTAL

Notes: Postage

Total

Name: Order No: Date of Order:

Address:

Date Placed:

Post ⬭   Collect ⬭   Deliver ⬭

Tracking No:

Contacted via: Paid Via:

Samples Sent:

⬭   ⬭   ⬭   ⬭   ⬭   ⬭   ⬭

PRODUCT	FRAGRANCE	QTY	TOTAL

Notes: Postage

Total

Name: Order No: Date of Order:

Address:

Post ⬭   Collect ⬭   Deliver ⬭   Date Placed:

Contacted via: Paid Via: Tracking No:

[Instagram] [Facebook] [Twitter] [Snapchat]   [PayPal] [Web] [Cash]

                                              Samples Sent:

⬭   ⬭   ⬭   ⬭   ⬭   ⬭   ⬭

PRODUCT	FRAGRANCE	QTY	TOTAL

Notes: Postage | |
                                          Total | |

Name: Order No: Date of Order:

Address:

Post ⬭   Collect ⬭   Deliver ⬭   Date Placed:

Contacted via: Paid Via: Tracking No:

[Instagram] [Facebook] [Twitter] [Snapchat]   [PayPal] [Web] [Cash]

                                              Samples Sent:

⬭   ⬭   ⬭   ⬭   ⬭   ⬭   ⬭

PRODUCT	FRAGRANCE	QTY	TOTAL

Notes: Postage | |
                                          Total | |

Name: Order No:

Address:

Post ⬭   Collect ⬭   Deliver ⬭

Contacted via: Paid Via:

⬭   ⬭   ⬭   ⬭   ⬭   ⬭   ⬭

Date of Order:

Date Placed:

Tracking No:

Samples Sent:

PRODUCT	FRAGRANCE	QTY	TOTAL

Notes: Postage | |
                                                    Total | |

Name: Order No:

Address:

Post ⬭   Collect ⬭   Deliver ⬭

Contacted via: Paid Via:

⬭   ⬭   ⬭   ⬭   ⬭   ⬭   ⬭

Date of Order:

Date Placed:

Tracking No:

Samples Sent:

PRODUCT	FRAGRANCE	QTY	TOTAL

Notes: Postage | |
                                                    Total | |

Name: Order No: Date of Order:

Address:

Post ◯   Collect ◯   Deliver ◯   Date Placed:

Contacted via: Paid Via: Tracking No:

Samples Sent:

◯   ◯   ◯   ◯   ◯   ◯   ◯

PRODUCT	FRAGRANCE	QTY	TOTAL

Notes:

	Postage	
	Total	

Name: Order No: Date of Order:

Address:

Post ◯   Collect ◯   Deliver ◯   Date Placed:

Contacted via: Paid Via: Tracking No:

Samples Sent:

◯   ◯   ◯   ◯   ◯   ◯   ◯

PRODUCT	FRAGRANCE	QTY	TOTAL

Notes:

	Postage	
	Total	

Name: Order No: Date of Order:

Address:
                                                Date Placed:
Post ◯   Collect ◯   Deliver ◯

Contacted via: Paid Via: Tracking No:

[Instagram] [Facebook] [Twitter] [Snapchat]   [PayPal] [Globe] [Cash]
                                                Samples Sent:
◯   ◯   ◯   ◯   ◯   ◯   ◯

PRODUCT	FRAGRANCE	QTY	TOTAL

Notes: Postage | |
                                        Total | |

Name: Order No: Date of Order:

Address:
                                                Date Placed:
Post ◯   Collect ◯   Deliver ◯

Contacted via: Paid Via: Tracking No:

[Instagram] [Facebook] [Twitter] [Snapchat]   [PayPal] [Globe] [Cash]

◯   ◯   ◯   ◯   ◯   ◯   ◯   Samples Sent:

PRODUCT	FRAGRANCE	QTY	TOTAL

Notes: Postage | |
                                        Total | |

Name: Order No: Date of Order:

Address:

Post ◯   Collect ◯   Deliver ◯   Date Placed:

Contacted via: **Paid Via:**   Tracking No:

[Instagram] [Facebook] [Twitter] [Snapchat]   [PayPal] [Globe] [Cash]

◯   ◯   ◯   ◯   ◯   ◯   ◯   Samples Sent:

PRODUCT	FRAGRANCE	QTY	TOTAL

Notes: Postage | |

Total | |

Name: Order No: Date of Order:

Address:

Post ◯   Collect ◯   Deliver ◯   Date Placed:

Contacted via: **Paid Via:**   Tracking No:

[Instagram] [Facebook] [Twitter] [Snapchat]   [PayPal] [Globe] [Cash]

◯   ◯   ◯   ◯   ◯   ◯   ◯   Samples Sent:

PRODUCT	FRAGRANCE	QTY	TOTAL

Notes: Postage | |

Total | |

Name:	Order No:	Date of Order:

Address:

Post ( )　　Collect ( )　　Deliver ( )

Date Placed:

Contacted via:　　　　　　　　Paid Via:

Tracking No:

Samples Sent:

PRODUCT	FRAGRANCE	QTY	TOTAL

Notes:

	Postage	
	Total	

Name:	Order No:	Date of Order:

Address:

Post ( )　　Collect ( )　　Deliver ( )

Date Placed:

Contacted via:　　　　　　　　Paid Via:

Tracking No:

Samples Sent:

PRODUCT	FRAGRANCE	QTY	TOTAL

Notes:

	Postage	
	Total	

Name: Order No: Date of Order:

Address:
                                                                            Date Placed:
Post ◯   Collect ◯   Deliver ◯

Contacted via: Paid Via: Tracking No:

[Instagram] [Facebook] [Twitter] [Snapchat]   [PayPal] [Globe] [Cash]

◯   ◯   ◯   ◯   ◯   ◯   ◯   Samples Sent:

PRODUCT	FRAGRANCE	QTY	TOTAL

Notes: Postage | |
                                                    Total | |

Name: Order No: Date of Order:

Address:
                                                                            Date Placed:
Post ◯   Collect ◯   Deliver ◯

Contacted via: Paid Via: Tracking No:

[Instagram] [Facebook] [Twitter] [Snapchat]   [PayPal] [Globe] [Cash]

◯   ◯   ◯   ◯   ◯   ◯   ◯   Samples Sent:

PRODUCT	FRAGRANCE	QTY	TOTAL

Notes: Postage | |
                                                    Total | |

		Order No:		Date of Order:

Name:

Order No:

Date of Order:

Address:

Date Placed:

Post ⬭ Collect ⬭ Deliver ⬭

Tracking No:

Contacted via: Paid Via:

⬭ ⬭ ⬭ ⬭   ⬭ ⬭ ⬭

Samples Sent:

PRODUCT	FRAGRANCE	QTY	TOTAL

Notes:

Postage	
Total	

Name:

Order No:

Date of Order:

Address:

Date Placed:

Post ⬭ Collect ⬭ Deliver ⬭

Tracking No:

Contacted via: Paid Via:

⬭ ⬭ ⬭ ⬭   ⬭ ⬭ ⬭

Samples Sent:

PRODUCT	FRAGRANCE	QTY	TOTAL

Notes:

Postage	
Total	

Name: Order No: Date of Order:

Address:
                                                      Date Placed:
Post ◯   Collect ◯   Deliver ◯

Contacted via: Paid Via: Tracking No:

[Instagram] [Facebook] [Twitter] [Snapchat]   [PayPal] [Globe] [Cash]

◯   ◯   ◯   ◯   ◯   ◯   ◯   Samples Sent:

PRODUCT	FRAGRANCE	QTY	TOTAL

Notes: Postage | |
                                                    Total | |

Name: Order No: Date of Order:

Address:
                                                      Date Placed:
Post ◯   Collect ◯   Deliver ◯

Contacted via: Paid Via: Tracking No:

[Instagram] [Facebook] [Twitter] [Snapchat]   [PayPal] [Globe] [Cash]

◯   ◯   ◯   ◯   ◯   ◯   ◯   Samples Sent:

PRODUCT	FRAGRANCE	QTY	TOTAL

Notes: Postage | |
                                                    Total | |

Name: Order No: Date of Order:

Address:

                                                        Date Placed:

Post ◯   Collect ◯   Deliver ◯

Contacted via: Paid Via: Tracking No:

◯   ◯   ◯   ◯   ◯   ◯   ◯   Samples Sent:

PRODUCT	FRAGRANCE	QTY	TOTAL

Notes: Postage

                                                    Total

Name: Order No: Date of Order:

Address:

                                                        Date Placed:

Post ◯   Collect ◯   Deliver ◯

Contacted via: Paid Via: Tracking No:

◯   ◯   ◯   ◯   ◯   ◯   ◯   Samples Sent:

PRODUCT	FRAGRANCE	QTY	TOTAL

Notes: Postage

                                                    Total

Name:		Order No:	Date of Order:
Address:			
Post ○ Collect ○ Deliver ○			Date Placed:
Contacted via:	Paid Via:		Tracking No:
			Samples Sent:
○ ○ ○ ○	○ ○ ○		

PRODUCT	FRAGRANCE	QTY	TOTAL

Notes:

Postage	
Total	

Name:		Order No:	Date of Order:
Address:			
Post ○ Collect ○ Deliver ○			Date Placed:
Contacted via:	Paid Via:		Tracking No:
			Samples Sent:
○ ○ ○ ○	○ ○ ○		

PRODUCT	FRAGRANCE	QTY	TOTAL

Notes:

Postage	
Total	

Name: Order No: | Date of Order:

Address:
                                                | Date Placed:
Post ◯   Collect ◯   Deliver ◯

Contacted via: Paid Via: | Tracking No:

[Instagram] [Facebook] [Twitter] [Snapchat]   [PayPal] [Globe] [Cash]

◯   ◯   ◯   ◯   ◯   ◯   ◯ | Samples Sent:

PRODUCT	FRAGRANCE	QTY	TOTAL

Notes: Postage | |
                                        Total | |

Name: Order No: | Date of Order:

Address:
                                                | Date Placed:
Post ◯   Collect ◯   Deliver ◯

Contacted via: Paid Via: | Tracking No:

[Instagram] [Facebook] [Twitter] [Snapchat]   [PayPal] [Globe] [Cash]

◯   ◯   ◯   ◯   ◯   ◯   ◯ | Samples Sent:

PRODUCT	FRAGRANCE	QTY	TOTAL

Notes: Postage | |
                                        Total | |

Name: Order No: Date of Order:

Address:
                                                      Date Placed:
Post ◯   Collect ◯   Deliver ◯

Contacted via: Paid Via: Tracking No:

[Instagram] [Facebook] [Twitter] [Snapchat]   [PayPal] [Globe] [Cash]   Samples Sent:
◯   ◯   ◯   ◯   ◯   ◯   ◯

PRODUCT	FRAGRANCE	QTY	TOTAL

Notes: Postage | |
                                                Total | |

Name: Order No: Date of Order:

Address:
                                                      Date Placed:
Post ◯   Collect ◯   Deliver ◯

Contacted via: Paid Via: Tracking No:

[Instagram] [Facebook] [Twitter] [Snapchat]   [PayPal] [Globe] [Cash]   Samples Sent:
◯   ◯   ◯   ◯   ◯   ◯   ◯

PRODUCT	FRAGRANCE	QTY	TOTAL

Notes: Postage | |
                                                Total | |

Order Form 1

Name: Order No: Date of Order:

Address:

Date Placed:

Post ◯   Collect ◯   Deliver ◯

Tracking No:

Contacted via: Paid Via:

Samples Sent:

Contacted via icons: Instagram ◯   Facebook ◯   Twitter ◯   Snapchat ◯

Paid Via icons: PayPal ◯   Web ◯   Cash ◯

PRODUCT	FRAGRANCE	QTY	TOTAL

Notes: Postage _____

Total _____

Order Form 2

Name: Order No: Date of Order:

Address:

Date Placed:

Post ◯   Collect ◯   Deliver ◯

Tracking No:

Contacted via: Paid Via:

Samples Sent:

Contacted via icons: Instagram ◯   Facebook ◯   Twitter ◯   Snapchat ◯

Paid Via icons: PayPal ◯   Web ◯   Cash ◯

PRODUCT	FRAGRANCE	QTY	TOTAL

Notes: Postage _____

Total _____

Name: **Order No:**   **Date of Order:**

Address:

Post ◯   Collect ◯   Deliver ◯   **Date Placed:**

Contacted via: **Paid Via:**   **Tracking No:**

[instagram] [facebook] [twitter] [snapchat]   [paypal] [globe] [cash]   **Samples Sent:**

◯   ◯   ◯   ◯   ◯   ◯   ◯

PRODUCT	FRAGRANCE	QTY	TOTAL

Notes: Postage

                                                     Total

Name: **Order No:**   **Date of Order:**

Address:

Post ◯   Collect ◯   Deliver ◯   **Date Placed:**

Contacted via: **Paid Via:**   **Tracking No:**

[instagram] [facebook] [twitter] [snapchat]   [paypal] [globe] [cash]   **Samples Sent:**

◯   ◯   ◯   ◯   ◯   ◯   ◯

PRODUCT	FRAGRANCE	QTY	TOTAL

Notes: Postage

                                                     Total

Name:		Order No:		Date of Order:
Address:				
Post ◯ Collect ◯ Deliver ◯				Date Placed:
Contacted via:	Paid Via:			Tracking No:
▢ f ▢ ▢	▢ ▢ ▢			Samples Sent:
◯ ◯ ◯ ◯	◯ ◯ ◯			

PRODUCT	FRAGRANCE	QTY	TOTAL

Notes:

Postage	
Total	

Name:		Order No:		Date of Order:
Address:				
Post ◯ Collect ◯ Deliver ◯				Date Placed:
Contacted via:	Paid Via:			Tracking No:
▢ f ▢ ▢	▢ ▢ ▢			Samples Sent:
◯ ◯ ◯ ◯	◯ ◯ ◯			

PRODUCT	FRAGRANCE	QTY	TOTAL

Notes:

Postage	
Total	

Name: Order No: Date of Order:

Address:

Date Placed:

Post ◯ Collect ◯ Deliver ◯

Contacted via: Paid Via: Tracking No:

Samples Sent:

◯ ◯ ◯ ◯ ◯ ◯ ◯

PRODUCT	FRAGRANCE	QTY	TOTAL

Notes: Postage

Total

Name: Order No: Date of Order:

Address:

Date Placed:

Post ◯ Collect ◯ Deliver ◯

Contacted via: Paid Via: Tracking No:

Samples Sent:

◯ ◯ ◯ ◯ ◯ ◯ ◯

PRODUCT	FRAGRANCE	QTY	TOTAL

Notes: Postage

Total

Name: Order No: Date of Order:

Address:
                                                      Date Placed:
Post ◯   Collect ◯   Deliver ◯

Contacted via: Paid Via: Tracking No:

[Instagram] [Facebook] [Twitter] [Snapchat]   [PayPal] [Globe] [Cash]   Samples Sent:
◯   ◯   ◯   ◯   ◯   ◯   ◯

PRODUCT	FRAGRANCE	QTY	TOTAL

Notes: Postage |
                                          Total |

Name: Order No: Date of Order:

Address:
                                                      Date Placed:
Post ◯   Collect ◯   Deliver ◯

Contacted via: Paid Via: Tracking No:

[Instagram] [Facebook] [Twitter] [Snapchat]   [PayPal] [Globe] [Cash]   Samples Sent:
◯   ◯   ◯   ◯   ◯   ◯   ◯

PRODUCT	FRAGRANCE	QTY	TOTAL

Notes: Postage |
                                          Total |

Name: Order No: Date of Order:

Address:
                                                            Date Placed:
Post ◯   Collect ◯   Deliver ◯

Contacted via: Paid Via: Tracking No:

[Instagram] [Facebook] [Twitter] [Snapchat]   [PayPal] [Globe] [Cash]

◯   ◯   ◯   ◯   ◯   ◯   ◯   Samples Sent:

PRODUCT	FRAGRANCE	QTY	TOTAL

Notes: Postage | |
                                                    Total | |

Name: Order No: Date of Order:

Address:
                                                            Date Placed:
Post ◯   Collect ◯   Deliver ◯

Contacted via: Paid Via: Tracking No:

[Instagram] [Facebook] [Twitter] [Snapchat]   [PayPal] [Globe] [Cash]

◯   ◯   ◯   ◯   ◯   ◯   ◯   Samples Sent:

PRODUCT	FRAGRANCE	QTY	TOTAL

Notes: Postage | |
                                                    Total | |

Name:	Order No:	Date of Order:
Address:		Date Placed:
Post ◯ Collect ◯ Deliver ◯		
Contacted via:	Paid Via:	Tracking No:
◯ ◯ ◯ ◯	◯ ◯ ◯	Samples Sent:

PRODUCT	FRAGRANCE	QTY	TOTAL

Notes:

Postage	
Total	

Name:	Order No:	Date of Order:
Address:		Date Placed:
Post ◯ Collect ◯ Deliver ◯		
Contacted via:	Paid Via:	Tracking No:
◯ ◯ ◯ ◯	◯ ◯ ◯	Samples Sent:

PRODUCT	FRAGRANCE	QTY	TOTAL

Notes:

Postage	
Total	

Name:		Order No:		Date of Order:

Address:

Post ◯   Collect ◯   Deliver ◯

Date Placed:

Contacted via: Paid Via:

Tracking No:

Samples Sent:

◯ ◯ ◯ ◯   ◯ ◯ ◯

PRODUCT	FRAGRANCE	QTY	TOTAL

Notes:

Postage	
Total	

Name:		Order No:		Date of Order:

Address:

Post ◯   Collect ◯   Deliver ◯

Date Placed:

Contacted via: Paid Via:

Tracking No:

Samples Sent:

◯ ◯ ◯ ◯   ◯ ◯ ◯

PRODUCT	FRAGRANCE	QTY	TOTAL

Notes:

Postage	
Total	

Name:		Order No:		Date of Order:

Address:

Post ⬭   Collect ⬭   Deliver ⬭

Date Placed:

Contacted via: Paid Via:

Tracking No:

Samples Sent:

⬭ ⬭ ⬭ ⬭   ⬭ ⬭ ⬭

PRODUCT	FRAGRANCE	QTY	TOTAL

Notes:

	Postage	
	Total	

Name:		Order No:		Date of Order:

Address:

Post ⬭   Collect ⬭   Deliver ⬭

Date Placed:

Contacted via: Paid Via:

Tracking No:

Samples Sent:

⬭ ⬭ ⬭ ⬭   ⬭ ⬭ ⬭

PRODUCT	FRAGRANCE	QTY	TOTAL

Notes:

	Postage	
	Total	

Name: Order No: Date of Order:

Address:

Date Placed:

Post ◯   Collect ◯   Deliver ◯

Contacted via: Paid Via:

Tracking No:

◯   ◯   ◯   ◯   ◯   ◯   ◯

Samples Sent:

PRODUCT	FRAGRANCE	QTY	TOTAL

Notes: Postage

Total

Name: Order No: Date of Order:

Address:

Date Placed:

Post ◯   Collect ◯   Deliver ◯

Contacted via: Paid Via:

Tracking No:

◯   ◯   ◯   ◯   ◯   ◯   ◯

Samples Sent:

PRODUCT	FRAGRANCE	QTY	TOTAL

Notes: Postage

Total

Name:	Order No:	Date of Order:
Address:		Date Placed:
Post ◯ Collect ◯ Deliver ◯		
Contacted via:	Paid Via:	Tracking No:
◯ ◯ ◯ ◯	◯ ◯ ◯	Samples Sent:

PRODUCT	FRAGRANCE	QTY	TOTAL

Notes:

Postage	
Total	

Name:	Order No:	Date of Order:
Address:		Date Placed:
Post ◯ Collect ◯ Deliver ◯		
Contacted via:	Paid Via:	Tracking No:
◯ ◯ ◯ ◯	◯ ◯ ◯	Samples Sent:

PRODUCT	FRAGRANCE	QTY	TOTAL

Notes:

Postage	
Total	

Name: **Order No:**   **Date of Order:**

Address:

Date Placed:

Post ◯   Collect ◯   Deliver ◯

Contacted via: **Paid Via:**   **Tracking No:**

◯ ◯ ◯ ◯   ◯ ◯ ◯

Samples Sent:

PRODUCT	FRAGRANCE	QTY	TOTAL

Notes: Postage

                                              Total

Name: **Order No:**   **Date of Order:**

Address:

Date Placed:

Post ◯   Collect ◯   Deliver ◯

Contacted via: **Paid Via:**   **Tracking No:**

◯ ◯ ◯ ◯   ◯ ◯ ◯

Samples Sent:

PRODUCT	FRAGRANCE	QTY	TOTAL

Notes: Postage

                                              Total

Name:	Order No:	Date of Order:
Address:		Date Placed:
Post ◯ Collect ◯ Deliver ◯		
Contacted via:	Paid Via:	Tracking No:
[Instagram] [Facebook] [Twitter] [Snapchat]	[PayPal] [Globe] [Cash]	Samples Sent:
◯ ◯ ◯ ◯	◯ ◯ ◯	

PRODUCT	FRAGRANCE	QTY	TOTAL

Notes:

Postage	
Total	

Name:	Order No:	Date of Order:
Address:		Date Placed:
Post ◯ Collect ◯ Deliver ◯		
Contacted via:	Paid Via:	Tracking No:
[Instagram] [Facebook] [Twitter] [Snapchat]	[PayPal] [Globe] [Cash]	Samples Sent:
◯ ◯ ◯ ◯	◯ ◯ ◯	

PRODUCT	FRAGRANCE	QTY	TOTAL

Notes:

Postage	
Total	

Name: Order No: Date of Order:

Address:

Date Placed:

Post ◯   Collect ◯   Deliver ◯

Contacted via: Paid Via: Tracking No:

Samples Sent:

◯   ◯   ◯   ◯   ◯   ◯   ◯

PRODUCT	FRAGRANCE	QTY	TOTAL

Notes: Postage

Total

Name: Order No: Date of Order:

Address:

Date Placed:

Post ◯   Collect ◯   Deliver ◯

Contacted via: Paid Via: Tracking No:

Samples Sent:

◯   ◯   ◯   ◯   ◯   ◯   ◯

PRODUCT	FRAGRANCE	QTY	TOTAL

Notes: Postage

Total

Name: Order No: Date of Order:

Address:
                                                      Date Placed:
Post ( )   Collect ( )   Deliver ( )

Contacted via: Paid Via: Tracking No:

[Instagram] [Facebook] [Twitter] [Snapchat]   [PayPal] [Globe] [Cash]
                                                      Samples Sent:
( )   ( )   ( )   ( )   ( )   ( )   ( )

PRODUCT	FRAGRANCE	QTY	TOTAL

Notes: Postage | |
                                            Total | |

Name: Order No: Date of Order:

Address:
                                                      Date Placed:
Post ( )   Collect ( )   Deliver ( )

Contacted via: Paid Via: Tracking No:

[Instagram] [Facebook] [Twitter] [Snapchat]   [PayPal] [Globe] [Cash]
                                                      Samples Sent:
( )   ( )   ( )   ( )   ( )   ( )   ( )

PRODUCT	FRAGRANCE	QTY	TOTAL

Notes: Postage | |
                                            Total | |

Name:	Order No:	Date of Order:

Address:

Post ◯   Collect ◯   Deliver ◯

Date Placed:

Contacted via: Paid Via:

Tracking No:

Samples Sent:

◯ ◯ ◯ ◯   ◯ ◯ ◯

PRODUCT	FRAGRANCE	QTY	TOTAL

Notes: Postage |

Total |

Name:	Order No:	Date of Order:

Address:

Post ◯   Collect ◯   Deliver ◯

Date Placed:

Contacted via: Paid Via:

Tracking No:

Samples Sent:

◯ ◯ ◯ ◯   ◯ ◯ ◯

PRODUCT	FRAGRANCE	QTY	TOTAL

Notes: Postage |

Total |

Order Form 1

Name: **Order No:**   **Date of Order:**

Address:

Date Placed:

Post ⬭   Collect ⬭   Deliver ⬭

Contacted via: **Paid Via:**   **Tracking No:**

[Instagram] [Facebook] [Twitter] [Snapchat]   [PayPal] [Globe] [Cash]

⬭   ⬭   ⬭   ⬭   ⬭   ⬭   ⬭   **Samples Sent:**

PRODUCT	FRAGRANCE	QTY	TOTAL

Notes: Postage | |

                   Total | |

Order Form 2

Name: **Order No:**   **Date of Order:**

Address:

Date Placed:

Post ⬭   Collect ⬭   Deliver ⬭

Contacted via: **Paid Via:**   **Tracking No:**

[Instagram] [Facebook] [Twitter] [Snapchat]   [PayPal] [Globe] [Cash]

⬭   ⬭   ⬭   ⬭   ⬭   ⬭   ⬭   **Samples Sent:**

PRODUCT	FRAGRANCE	QTY	TOTAL

Notes: Postage | |

                   Total | |

Name: Order No: Date of Order:

Address:
                                                        Date Placed:
Post ◯   Collect ◯   Deliver ◯

Contacted via: Paid Via: Tracking No:

[Instagram] [Facebook] [Twitter] [Snapchat]   [PayPal] [Globe] [Cash]

                                                        Samples Sent:

◯   ◯   ◯   ◯   ◯   ◯   ◯

PRODUCT	FRAGRANCE	QTY	TOTAL

Notes: Postage | |
                                                Total | |

Name: Order No: Date of Order:

Address:
                                                        Date Placed:
Post ◯   Collect ◯   Deliver ◯

Contacted via: Paid Via: Tracking No:

[Instagram] [Facebook] [Twitter] [Snapchat]   [PayPal] [Globe] [Cash]

                                                        Samples Sent:

◯   ◯   ◯   ◯   ◯   ◯   ◯

PRODUCT	FRAGRANCE	QTY	TOTAL

Notes: Postage | |
                                                Total | |

Name:		Order No:	Date of Order:
Address:			Date Placed:
Post ◯ Collect ◯ Deliver ◯			
Contacted via:	Paid Via:		Tracking No:
📷 f 🐦 👻	P 🌐 💵		Samples Sent:
◯ ◯ ◯ ◯	◯ ◯ ◯		

PRODUCT	FRAGRANCE	QTY	TOTAL

Notes:

Postage	
Total	

Name:		Order No:	Date of Order:
Address:			Date Placed:
Post ◯ Collect ◯ Deliver ◯			
Contacted via:	Paid Via:		Tracking No:
📷 f 🐦 👻	P 🌐 💵		Samples Sent:
◯ ◯ ◯ ◯	◯ ◯ ◯		

PRODUCT	FRAGRANCE	QTY	TOTAL

Notes:

Postage	
Total	

Name: **Order No:**   **Date of Order:**

Address:

Date Placed:

Post ◯   Collect ◯   Deliver ◯

Contacted via: **Paid Via:**   **Tracking No:**

◯   ◯   ◯   ◯   ◯   ◯   ◯   **Samples Sent:**

PRODUCT	FRAGRANCE	QTY	TOTAL

Notes: **Postage**

Total

Name: **Order No:**   **Date of Order:**

Address:

Date Placed:

Post ◯   Collect ◯   Deliver ◯

Contacted via: **Paid Via:**   **Tracking No:**

◯   ◯   ◯   ◯   ◯   ◯   ◯   **Samples Sent:**

PRODUCT	FRAGRANCE	QTY	TOTAL

Notes: **Postage**

Total

	Name:	Order No:	Date of Order:

Name:

Order No:

Date of Order:

Address:

Date Placed:

Post ⬭ Collect ⬭ Deliver ⬭

Contacted via: **Paid Via:**

Tracking No:

⬭ ⬭ ⬭ ⬭   ⬭ ⬭ ⬭

Samples Sent:

PRODUCT	FRAGRANCE	QTY	TOTAL

Notes: Postage

                                                Total

Name: **Order No:**   **Date of Order:**

Address:

Date Placed:

Post ⬭ Collect ⬭ Deliver ⬭

Contacted via: **Paid Via:**

Tracking No:

⬭ ⬭ ⬭ ⬭   ⬭ ⬭ ⬭

Samples Sent:

PRODUCT	FRAGRANCE	QTY	TOTAL

Notes: Postage

                                                Total

Name:	Order No:	Date of Order:

Address:

Post ◯   Collect ◯   Deliver ◯

Date Placed:

Contacted via: Paid Via:

Tracking No:

Samples Sent:

◯ ◯ ◯ ◯   ◯ ◯ ◯

PRODUCT	FRAGRANCE	QTY	TOTAL

Notes:

	Postage	
	Total	

Name:	Order No:	Date of Order:

Address:

Post ◯   Collect ◯   Deliver ◯

Date Placed:

Contacted via: Paid Via:

Tracking No:

Samples Sent:

◯ ◯ ◯ ◯   ◯ ◯ ◯

PRODUCT	FRAGRANCE	QTY	TOTAL

Notes:

	Postage	
	Total	

Name:	Order No:	Date of Order:
Address:		Date Placed:
Post ◯ Collect ◯ Deliver ◯		
Contacted via:	Paid Via:	Tracking No:
�(Instagram) (Facebook) (Twitter) (Snapchat)	(PayPal) (Globe) (Cash)	Samples Sent:
◯ ◯ ◯ ◯	◯ ◯ ◯	

PRODUCT	FRAGRANCE	QTY	TOTAL

Notes:

Postage	
Total	

Name:	Order No:	Date of Order:
Address:		Date Placed:
Post ◯ Collect ◯ Deliver ◯		
Contacted via:	Paid Via:	Tracking No:
(Instagram) (Facebook) (Twitter) (Snapchat)	(PayPal) (Globe) (Cash)	Samples Sent:
◯ ◯ ◯ ◯	◯ ◯ ◯	

PRODUCT	FRAGRANCE	QTY	TOTAL

Notes:

Postage	
Total	

Name: Order No: Date of Order:

Address:
                                                            Date Placed:
Post ◯   Collect ◯   Deliver ◯

Contacted via: Paid Via: Tracking No:

📷 f 🐦 👻   P 🌐 💵   Samples Sent:

◯   ◯   ◯   ◯   ◯   ◯   ◯

PRODUCT	FRAGRANCE	QTY	TOTAL

Notes: Postage | |
                                                  Total | |

Name: Order No: Date of Order:

Address:
                                                            Date Placed:
Post ◯   Collect ◯   Deliver ◯

Contacted via: Paid Via: Tracking No:

📷 f 🐦 👻   P 🌐 💵   Samples Sent:

◯   ◯   ◯   ◯   ◯   ◯   ◯

PRODUCT	FRAGRANCE	QTY	TOTAL

Notes: Postage | |
                                                  Total | |

Name:		Order No:		Date of Order:

Address:

Post ◯ Collect ◯ Deliver ◯

Date Placed:

Contacted via: Paid Via:

Tracking No:

Samples Sent:

◯ ◯ ◯ ◯   ◯ ◯ ◯

PRODUCT	FRAGRANCE	QTY	TOTAL

Notes:

Postage	
Total	

Name:		Order No:		Date of Order:

Address:

Post ◯ Collect ◯ Deliver ◯

Date Placed:

Contacted via: Paid Via:

Tracking No:

Samples Sent:

◯ ◯ ◯ ◯   ◯ ◯ ◯

PRODUCT	FRAGRANCE	QTY	TOTAL

Notes:

Postage	
Total	

Name: Order No: Date of Order:

Address:
                                                      Date Placed:
Post ⬭   Collect ⬭   Deliver ⬭

Contacted via: Paid Via: Tracking No:

[Instagram] [Facebook] [Twitter] [Snapchat]   [PayPal] [Globe] [Cash]

⬭   ⬭   ⬭   ⬭   ⬭   ⬭   ⬭   Samples Sent:

PRODUCT	FRAGRANCE	QTY	TOTAL

Notes: Postage | |
                                                Total | |

Name: Order No: Date of Order:

Address:
                                                      Date Placed:
Post ⬭   Collect ⬭   Deliver ⬭

Contacted via: Paid Via: Tracking No:

[Instagram] [Facebook] [Twitter] [Snapchat]   [PayPal] [Globe] [Cash]

⬭   ⬭   ⬭   ⬭   ⬭   ⬭   ⬭   Samples Sent:

PRODUCT	FRAGRANCE	QTY	TOTAL

Notes: Postage | |
                                                Total | |

Name:	Order No:	Date of Order:
Address:		Date Placed:

Post ⬭ Collect ⬭ Deliver ⬭

Contacted via:	Paid Via:	Tracking No:

⬭ ⬭ ⬭ ⬭   ⬭ ⬭ ⬭

Samples Sent:

PRODUCT	FRAGRANCE	QTY	TOTAL

Notes:

	Postage	
	Total	

Name:	Order No:	Date of Order:
Address:		Date Placed:

Post ⬭ Collect ⬭ Deliver ⬭

Contacted via:	Paid Via:	Tracking No:

⬭ ⬭ ⬭ ⬭   ⬭ ⬭ ⬭

Samples Sent:

PRODUCT	FRAGRANCE	QTY	TOTAL

Notes:

	Postage	
	Total	

Name: Order No: Date of Order:

Address:

Post ◯   Collect ◯   Deliver ◯   Date Placed:

Contacted via: Paid Via: Tracking No:

[Instagram] [Facebook] [Twitter] [Snapchat]   [PayPal] [Web] [Cash]

◯   ◯   ◯   ◯   ◯   ◯   ◯   Samples Sent:

PRODUCT	FRAGRANCE	QTY	TOTAL

Notes: Postage | |

                                                        Total | |

Name: Order No: Date of Order:

Address:

Post ◯   Collect ◯   Deliver ◯   Date Placed:

Contacted via: Paid Via: Tracking No:

[Instagram] [Facebook] [Twitter] [Snapchat]   [PayPal] [Web] [Cash]

◯   ◯   ◯   ◯   ◯   ◯   ◯   Samples Sent:

PRODUCT	FRAGRANCE	QTY	TOTAL

Notes: Postage | |

                                                        Total | |

Name: Order No: Date of Order:

Address:

Post ◯   Collect ◯   Deliver ◯   Date Placed:

Contacted via: Paid Via: Tracking No:

◯   ◯   ◯   ◯   ◯   ◯   ◯   Samples Sent:

PRODUCT	FRAGRANCE	QTY	TOTAL

Notes: Postage |
                                              Total |

Name: Order No: Date of Order:

Address:

Post ◯   Collect ◯   Deliver ◯   Date Placed:

Contacted via: Paid Via: Tracking No:

◯   ◯   ◯   ◯   ◯   ◯   ◯   Samples Sent:

PRODUCT	FRAGRANCE	QTY	TOTAL

Notes: Postage |
                                              Total |

Order Form 1

Name: Order No: Date of Order:

Address:

Post ◯   Collect ◯   Deliver ◯   Date Placed:

Contacted via: Paid Via: Tracking No:

[Instagram] [Facebook] [Twitter] [Snapchat]   [PayPal] [Web] [Cash]

◯   ◯   ◯   ◯   ◯   ◯   ◯   Samples Sent:

PRODUCT	FRAGRANCE	QTY	TOTAL

Notes: Postage

                          Total

Order Form 2

Name: Order No: Date of Order:

Address:

Post ◯   Collect ◯   Deliver ◯   Date Placed:

Contacted via: Paid Via: Tracking No:

[Instagram] [Facebook] [Twitter] [Snapchat]   [PayPal] [Web] [Cash]

◯   ◯   ◯   ◯   ◯   ◯   ◯   Samples Sent:

PRODUCT	FRAGRANCE	QTY	TOTAL

Notes: Postage

                          Total

Name: Order No: Date of Order:

Address:

Post ◯   Collect ◯   Deliver ◯   Date Placed:

Contacted via: Paid Via: Tracking No:

                   Samples Sent:

◯   ◯   ◯   ◯   ◯   ◯   ◯

PRODUCT	FRAGRANCE	QTY	TOTAL

Notes: Postage

                                          Total

Name: Order No: Date of Order:

Address:

Post ◯   Collect ◯   Deliver ◯   Date Placed:

Contacted via: Paid Via: Tracking No:

                   Samples Sent:

◯   ◯   ◯   ◯   ◯   ◯   ◯

PRODUCT	FRAGRANCE	QTY	TOTAL

Notes: Postage

                                          Total

Name: Order No: Date of Order:

Address:
                                                      Date Placed:
Post ◯   Collect ◯   Deliver ◯

Contacted via: Paid Via: Tracking No:

[Instagram] [Facebook] [Twitter] [Snapchat]   [PayPal] [Web] [Cash]
                                                      Samples Sent:
◯   ◯   ◯   ◯   ◯   ◯   ◯

PRODUCT	FRAGRANCE	QTY	TOTAL

Notes: Postage | |
                                              Total | |

Name: Order No: Date of Order:

Address:
                                                      Date Placed:
Post ◯   Collect ◯   Deliver ◯

Contacted via: Paid Via: Tracking No:

[Instagram] [Facebook] [Twitter] [Snapchat]   [PayPal] [Web] [Cash]
                                                      Samples Sent:
◯   ◯   ◯   ◯   ◯   ◯   ◯

PRODUCT	FRAGRANCE	QTY	TOTAL

Notes: Postage | |
                                              Total | |

Name:		Order No:		Date of Order:
Address:				
Post ◯　Collect ◯　Deliver ◯				Date Placed:
Contacted via:	Paid Via:			Tracking No:
(icons) ◯ ◯ ◯ ◯	(icons) ◯ ◯ ◯			Samples Sent:

PRODUCT	FRAGRANCE	QTY	TOTAL

Notes:

	Postage	
	Total	

Name:		Order No:		Date of Order:
Address:				
Post ◯　Collect ◯　Deliver ◯				Date Placed:
Contacted via:	Paid Via:			Tracking No:
(icons) ◯ ◯ ◯ ◯	(icons) ◯ ◯ ◯			Samples Sent:

PRODUCT	FRAGRANCE	QTY	TOTAL

Notes:

	Postage	
	Total	

Name:		Order No:	Date of Order:

Address:

Post ⬭ Collect ⬭ Deliver ⬭

Contacted via: Paid Via:

Date Placed:

Tracking No:

Samples Sent:

⬭ ⬭ ⬭ ⬭   ⬭ ⬭ ⬭

PRODUCT	FRAGRANCE	QTY	TOTAL

Notes:

	Postage	
	Total	

Name:		Order No:	Date of Order:

Address:

Post ⬭ Collect ⬭ Deliver ⬭

Contacted via: Paid Via:

Date Placed:

Tracking No:

Samples Sent:

⬭ ⬭ ⬭ ⬭   ⬭ ⬭ ⬭

PRODUCT	FRAGRANCE	QTY	TOTAL

Notes:

	Postage	
	Total	

Name:	Order No:	Date of Order:
Address:		Date Placed:
Post ⬭ Collect ⬭ Deliver ⬭		
Contacted via:	Paid Via:	Tracking No:
📷 f 🐦 👻	P 🌐 💵	Samples Sent:
⬭ ⬭ ⬭ ⬭	⬭ ⬭ ⬭	

PRODUCT	FRAGRANCE	QTY	TOTAL
Notes:		Postage	
		Total	

Name:	Order No:	Date of Order:
Address:		Date Placed:
Post ⬭ Collect ⬭ Deliver ⬭		
Contacted via:	Paid Via:	Tracking No:
📷 f 🐦 👻	P 🌐 💵	Samples Sent:
⬭ ⬭ ⬭ ⬭	⬭ ⬭ ⬭	

PRODUCT	FRAGRANCE	QTY	TOTAL
Notes:		Postage	
		Total	

Name:	Order No:	Date of Order:

Address:

Post ⬭ Collect ⬭ Deliver ⬭

Date Placed:

Contacted via:　　　　　　　　Paid Via:

Tracking No:

⬭ ⬭ ⬭ ⬭　　　⬭ ⬭ ⬭

Samples Sent:

PRODUCT	FRAGRANCE	QTY	TOTAL

Notes:

	Postage	
	Total	

Name:	Order No:	Date of Order:

Address:

Post ⬭ Collect ⬭ Deliver ⬭

Date Placed:

Contacted via:　　　　　　　　Paid Via:

Tracking No:

⬭ ⬭ ⬭ ⬭　　　⬭ ⬭ ⬭

Samples Sent:

PRODUCT	FRAGRANCE	QTY	TOTAL

Notes:

	Postage	
	Total	

Name:		Order No:	Date of Order:
Address:			Date Placed:
Post ◯ Collect ◯ Deliver ◯			
Contacted via:	Paid Via:		Tracking No:
[Instagram] [Facebook] [Twitter] [Snapchat]	[PayPal] [Globe] [Cash]		Samples Sent:
◯ ◯ ◯ ◯	◯ ◯ ◯		

PRODUCT	FRAGRANCE	QTY	TOTAL

Notes:

Postage	
Total	

Name:		Order No:	Date of Order:
Address:			Date Placed:
Post ◯ Collect ◯ Deliver ◯			
Contacted via:	Paid Via:		Tracking No:
[Instagram] [Facebook] [Twitter] [Snapchat]	[PayPal] [Globe] [Cash]		Samples Sent:
◯ ◯ ◯ ◯	◯ ◯ ◯		

PRODUCT	FRAGRANCE	QTY	TOTAL

Notes:

Postage	
Total	

Name:		Order No:		Date of Order:

Address:

Post ◯   Collect ◯   Deliver ◯

Date Placed:

Contacted via: Paid Via:

Tracking No:

Samples Sent:

◯ ◯ ◯ ◯   ◯ ◯ ◯

PRODUCT	FRAGRANCE	QTY	TOTAL

Notes: Postage

Total

Name:		Order No:		Date of Order:

Address:

Post ◯   Collect ◯   Deliver ◯

Date Placed:

Contacted via: Paid Via:

Tracking No:

Samples Sent:

◯ ◯ ◯ ◯   ◯ ◯ ◯

PRODUCT	FRAGRANCE	QTY	TOTAL

Notes: Postage

Total

Name:		Order No:	Date of Order:
Address:			Date Placed:
Post ◯ Collect ◯ Deliver ◯			
Contacted via:	Paid Via:		Tracking No:
			Samples Sent:

PRODUCT	FRAGRANCE	QTY	TOTAL

Notes:

Postage	
Total	

Name:		Order No:	Date of Order:
Address:			Date Placed:
Post ◯ Collect ◯ Deliver ◯			
Contacted via:	Paid Via:		Tracking No:
			Samples Sent:

PRODUCT	FRAGRANCE	QTY	TOTAL

Notes:

Postage	
Total	

Name: Order No: Date of Order:

Address:
                                                      Date Placed:
Post ◯   Collect ◯   Deliver ◯

Contacted via: Paid Via: Tracking No:

[Instagram] [f] [Twitter] [Snapchat]   [P] [Globe] [$]

◯   ◯   ◯   ◯   ◯   ◯   ◯   Samples Sent:

PRODUCT	FRAGRANCE	QTY	TOTAL

Notes: Postage

                                           Total

Name: Order No: Date of Order:

Address:
                                                      Date Placed:
Post ◯   Collect ◯   Deliver ◯

Contacted via: Paid Via: Tracking No:

[Instagram] [f] [Twitter] [Snapchat]   [P] [Globe] [$]

◯   ◯   ◯   ◯   ◯   ◯   ◯   Samples Sent:

PRODUCT	FRAGRANCE	QTY	TOTAL

Notes: Postage

                                           Total

Name:		Order No:		Date of Order:

Address:

Post ◯   Collect ◯   Deliver ◯

Date Placed:

Contacted via: Paid Via:

Tracking No:

Samples Sent:

◯ ◯ ◯ ◯   ◯ ◯ ◯

PRODUCT	FRAGRANCE	QTY	TOTAL

Notes:

Postage	
Total	

Name:		Order No:		Date of Order:

Address:

Post ◯   Collect ◯   Deliver ◯

Date Placed:

Contacted via: Paid Via:

Tracking No:

Samples Sent:

◯ ◯ ◯ ◯   ◯ ◯ ◯

PRODUCT	FRAGRANCE	QTY	TOTAL

Notes:

Postage	
Total	

Name: Order No: Date of Order:

Address:
                                                                Date Placed:
Post ◯   Collect ◯   Deliver ◯

Contacted via: Paid Via: Tracking No:

◻ ◻ ◻ ◻   ◻ ◻ ◻   Samples Sent:

◯ ◯ ◯ ◯   ◯ ◯ ◯

PRODUCT	FRAGRANCE	QTY	TOTAL

Notes: Postage | |
                                                  Total | |

Name: Order No: Date of Order:

Address:
                                                                Date Placed:
Post ◯   Collect ◯   Deliver ◯

Contacted via: Paid Via: Tracking No:

◻ ◻ ◻ ◻   ◻ ◻ ◻   Samples Sent:

◯ ◯ ◯ ◯   ◯ ◯ ◯

PRODUCT	FRAGRANCE	QTY	TOTAL

Notes: Postage | |
                                                  Total | |

Name:		Order No:	Date of Order:

Address:

Post ⬭   Collect ⬭   Deliver ⬭

Date Placed:

Contacted via: Paid Via:

Tracking No:

⬭ ⬭ ⬭ ⬭   ⬭ ⬭ ⬭

Samples Sent:

PRODUCT	FRAGRANCE	QTY	TOTAL

Notes:

	Postage	
	Total	

Name:		Order No:	Date of Order:

Address:

Post ⬭   Collect ⬭   Deliver ⬭

Date Placed:

Contacted via: Paid Via:

Tracking No:

⬭ ⬭ ⬭ ⬭   ⬭ ⬭ ⬭

Samples Sent:

PRODUCT	FRAGRANCE	QTY	TOTAL

Notes:

	Postage	
	Total	

Name:		Order No:	Date of Order:
Address:			
Post ◯ Collect ◯ Deliver ◯			Date Placed:
Contacted via:	Paid Via:		Tracking No:
📷 f 🐦 👻	🅿 🌐 💵		Samples Sent:
◯ ◯ ◯ ◯	◯ ◯ ◯		

PRODUCT	FRAGRANCE	QTY	TOTAL
Notes:		Postage	
		Total	

Name:		Order No:	Date of Order:
Address:			
Post ◯ Collect ◯ Deliver ◯			Date Placed:
Contacted via:	Paid Via:		Tracking No:
📷 f 🐦 👻	🅿 🌐 💵		Samples Sent:
◯ ◯ ◯ ◯	◯ ◯ ◯		

PRODUCT	FRAGRANCE	QTY	TOTAL
Notes:		Postage	
		Total	

Name:		Order No:		Date of Order:
Address:				
Post ◯ Collect ◯ Deliver ◯				Date Placed:
Contacted via:		Paid Via:		Tracking No:
◯ ◯ ◯ ◯		◯ ◯ ◯		Samples Sent:

PRODUCT	FRAGRANCE	QTY	TOTAL

Notes:

		Postage	
		Total	

Name:		Order No:		Date of Order:
Address:				
Post ◯ Collect ◯ Deliver ◯				Date Placed:
Contacted via:		Paid Via:		Tracking No:
◯ ◯ ◯ ◯		◯ ◯ ◯		Samples Sent:

PRODUCT	FRAGRANCE	QTY	TOTAL

Notes:

		Postage	
		Total	

Printed in Great Britain
by Amazon